Words for the Dead

Lake Angela

FUTURECYCLE PRESS
www.futurecycle.org

Cover image, *"Das Ungeborene und die Amsel,"* a composite
by Lake Angela based on the sonogram of her first lost child;
author photo by Tanne Willow; cover and interior book design
by Diane Kistner; ITC Cerigo text and titling

Library of Congress Control Number: 2020947070

Published by FutureCycle Press
Athens, Georgia, USA

ISBN 978-1-952593-04-8

for Spencer A. Parker (1990-2014)
and my dead children

69 | When the *products of conception* crush out,
70 | I begin to tell you the bedtime story again,
     and you are dead now.
70 | The time has come and come.
70 | The birds came up in order. The oldest and youngest
70 | I dreamed I was you

The dead don't need them.
They have something much more
potent than my words and yours
multiplied: movement.
Their mouths transmogrify
gold-foil coins into decay—
a rush of yellow flowers
so their soles go on glowing
underwater slowed to gleaming
adoration, violet prayer—
but they bless us with their names,
and so it is we walk with rivers
underneath transforming corpses:
cold flames of our drowned
points becoming stars.

The birds of prey have gathered together.
Bear your fractured collection of driftwood,
build yourself a coffin, gathered in sunrise.
You may rise in search of lost colors,
but you must also change your death.

My cold lips have always been blue.
Trapdoors hide in the corners of childhood
pictures. Lake in the mouth, sand in the lungs,
spring in the background, a porcelain
corpse in the foreground.
The focus is a black string.

Before memory a child is black and white.
Her halation kneels before stone.
A holy corpse drips red flowers
from her limbs, fingertips soft as blood.
Her bright head crowned by hornets, she gives
them the history of roses, the fragrance
that compels them to attack. You can hear them
above her heaven-raised eyes, droning
what they read in the rotting fruits.

Almost despite the cold earth, the frozen ridge
of dirt, the frost, the bones gleaming from corpse
toys, the blue lips—a bird is born between
broken memories, from a yellowed mouth
breaks forth and freezes.

At the funeral they open the box
full of shining metal
and try to feed the fish on slices of light—
orange beads, dark blue glass, yellow
to lure the eyeless on fragmented luster
like a promise without a shadow.

It starts with the feeling of gratitude
for those who eat me, ghosts who slowly turn
life to life, then the hard work of extracting

this bright, cold clean from my entrails
so unlike the warm layer of dirt that comforts
the skin or the bright dust of my young
thoughts scattered on earth, decaying
furrows, the colors of air quivering unseen,
the pulsing love the fingertips express
for the throat, the way the darknesses weave
through blue as though marriage
were a matter for rivers and shadow
rather than rivers driven through
shadow by something
other

unstill like a small, living creature
you believe you recognize rocking
on familiar carpet, a fetus unnamed
or unnameable that rises like a cloud
of dust from the strands of your hair,
from the light overhead, from the fixture
that breaks and suspends—
midlight.

It starts—to stir under my stomach.
I do not want to do the things
not worth making, a painting, a painting—

from sounds we take those sensations
that convey perhaps
we were alive. Words know me.

I have another body now;
my poetry body left as the music moved
the limbs we had abandoned a long way back.

Here we are.

How to negotiate
with silence—

it is unnecessary. Everyone knows we are neither
as young nor attractive as we hope, as we build
our grammars upon, our towers.

It was new to me that I cannot be a nun simply because
I do not believe in the God nuns now must know:

the God of man

even though that God claims
to know me.
You still have my mind

my snow in blue light, the darkest memory
of my cold as it rises from all memories,
from childhood, the frostbitten mind
of younger shapes, the membranes of night,
the stars assassinated for our sake:

for our fathers
and forefathers
hunted, stalked us

in our silken sleeps,
marked us with gold
paint and cries that fade.
We cannot afford the bodies that last.
We have no dance powerful enough
to drive forever back.

As we decompose
we watch the clouds pass on.

We observe everything
but the motion welling within,
preparing us to move anthills
grain by grain, to recoil in orange-
bronze undulations the sensation
of minute millions of legs
prowling deeper, searching the skin
for what world was there.

Everyone I have loved—
Name
Name
Poems:
the sound stripped from bowed strings
flung loose in harsh winds
and salt
—and who knows me from within
drowns in Lake waters
all white with feathers, so white.

The turmoil of dashing the brain
and blood to white bone on brown rocks:
that is how we were composed—in love.

Everyone I love—composites of color—
hears their exhales and follows
over the sighs of small earthquakes,
stumbling upon the voice I lost
in the Lake
and the planet they misplaced
for the moment.

The making and keeping of promises is a business
like excess road, an unhinged mouth swollen with fever
and disguised as lavender.

Half-buried on the shoulder, a grotesque face
gapes in filth with violet lips.

When I was at war in a childhood
beyond trees, I remember the angel
who drugged me. She was pristine.
She had no face.

All ways of considering the musculature
point to the north, the boat moored
to the tree, the invisible rope.

Why is the most beautiful
the superlative failure?

＊

When I was a child, I lived
in the cold. Blizzard adorned
my hair, pierced through—
I could feel clearly
as frozen eyes see sharply,
as blue stars,
as far as calm,
as the dead before the storm.

＊

She stormed, shaking the shadows
of solid objects with her teeth.
In the eye of the angerstorm,
or some time before, she forgot
they are alive also. The angels' red
fur ripped to flakes drifts light
fluff like snow. A flight of black
eagles blizzards, always falling,
never fallen. Before all, it is the tree
who knows; after all, in the quiet
light of the yellow room,
the children go on playing,
dead snakes on the dusty floor.

The doors to the rooms hang open now,
bared to light and protecting no one.
The snow illuminates from underneath.
Sparse tracks remain where solitary rabbits
have crossed light and shadow to meet themselves
at the summit: elder bush snapped
by snowy weight, warped lace of evergreen
shades cast like fans of chilled teeth.

Perhaps the travelers did not see their way
composed of the cross of shadow and light
but perceived the intersection instead
and followed the gradations of absence
to a summit—not a place you have loved,
not the snow of our childhood where
the absence of absence is love.

Remember the stories I read you?
The book prescribed tormented us both.
The textures of those nights
were never photographed.
I remember you then as well.

A blanket of snow will keep you
safe: intact, obscured.

My photographs of you are from far away,
distant grains of the childhood you distrusted
as ghosts, as holiness, the flower in the father's
white coat pocket.

I mourn you with my eyes in the mouth
we disliked. I did not know you were there. I did not know
who died first.

In another negative I come to know a sea, the swells,
a gull, a man clothed in blue to please me, to hide me.

Come to know; we do not converse but smile
to each other's eyes, each other's distant homes, crossed.
We come to look alike

as you fade, forward or back, old ghosts, whether white fog
or snow. I left you there in that frightening cold.

I can't hear you over the ice.
Don't say beautiful things to me.

As it turned out, his guardian angel
had a deep, malarial voice. The priest,
as sick as his secrets, lying in his robes

the color of cleaner blood, looked forward
to the resurrection of the dead he used to know.
The night keeps this silence beautiful
like the virus inside the blood. The word
only exits his mouth, never enters. "Lord,
I am not worthy for you to enter me, but"
the casino rings red and vibrant downstairs,
like a dream that cannot end without a death.

I found my body before, collected it
from the corpse of words, ready to resurrect
without a story this time. The great, lost bees
swarm and love me with their black buzzing,
wings waving a rapid darkness to depths
more complex than a son, depths less complex
than love from the hard, black bees of loss.

Why must the canary labor in the mine?
The human creation is a poison betrayal.

When I find the perfect word—from blood and dirt
or dreams of my death—I will make our child from it.

What if it is a name that cannot be spoken, only
emoted? Ask her to show me to the mirror, behind
a small, yellow door, where I lift whiskey to my lips
and those of my dead brother. The family on the other
side masticates, and my reflection is quiet and sallow,
behind it the higher head of my brother in bright white.
Cheers to you who shared my childhood sorrow.
We drank it then. It tastes stronger, more familiar, now.

It is like a song you told me had been sung differently before.
When I returned to my childhood home, each church sang
you a funeral—far from our glowing hives of black bees,
rainstreaked leaves and severed limbs, devout ants
slowly collecting their offerings, and on. If you are right
and the words were never in tune, we were slightly drunk
all childhood.

Imprinted on the tide is a place before
waking, where we are still dead until daybreak—
the crosses of blue over precious metals.

The same black strength
in yes and no pours from hours
all fluids into a foreign place.

The ants crawl up and down the shape.

The experiment is better
if we fail a lot.
The memory is better
if documented in German,
or sitting in a sandbox
playing with the words,

"Why did you let him die?
I had to. I'm not as kind as time,"
seeing visions
not meant for my fingertips.

In reality I remember inversely—
and I cannot step in water, only sky.

But how sad—a childhood wasted
in this particular way: on looking
at lace rather than through lace
when the wings of the yellow jacket
rise or the fine veins of the leaf touch
the stream and muted lips, there,

there. The more sorrow augments
the water concealed in crops,
weighing upon the farmer's crooked
back and unwieldy with the stoned
fruits, the faster the inhabitants
of this country multiply the dead.
They grasp the figs to bury
in the swollen earth when they are still
fresh, ripe, violet, and sweet. Dying

seems interesting. It is the thought
of being dead that frightens us.

From my mouth drop more densely
in autumn, as always, small leaves:
bright poems for those who can read
foliage. Maybe it is time
I learn to breathe.

It is an airtight trapeze filled
with the choicest abuses, fond
of the violence upon the violets grown
upon the open grave. My mother's
country holds a parade for the dead
with blue eyes, the fallen waves,
those with bruised faces, the bodies
of words that horrify the prisons
and set the bars convulsing.

The bones in my body bend,
and harrowing jaws set out a soft bird
so easily crushed by wind or by hand—

but perhaps we will make it back
to the water this time. At the Lake's
sudden edge stands a grave voice,
a grave, a madman spewing water
from his eyes; only a madman
is a flying fish. Only a madman escapes.

I am hiding behind words—
I already have said it all once.
The words—like fallen teeth, or the stars
we used to see from here—are the bones
of imaginary shapes, shining abscesses,
the grave-markers of long-rotted meats.

To measure love in digestion, in cattle,
in rest, without—what will become
of the internal landscapes? How to distribute
the love that will flow from the heart
without end once severed? Like the deep
sea fish who dies of decompression, the rupture
of the eye signifies the vision of this world,
the hands stolen and stuffed in the pockets
like change. Fed on their sisters unknowing,
complicit in emptying the sky of faces,
as long as one rat is crushed in the harvest,
men must hold themselves. They must
not be others, must not be called cannibals.

The anxiety of waking beside a certain horizon
effects shadows, thoughts inside a cannon.
Men laud the invention of rain. Our sorrow

is there: inside the slender shoot of a flower;
a blooming voice is a blooming arrow,
a terrified sleep. A helplessness is strewn
alongside so many sprawling garden weeds,
now wildly overgrown, like our ancestors
who come here when they forget
their voices because they all stopped singing
the songs. Uninvited themselves, they bring guests.

The shadowbody of antlers dusted in velvet
and darkness throws a long tunnel. A row
of poplars sinks in shades, venomless
skates. Someone has stepped back onto the boat
and forgotten, swaying in the sea of ghosts—
one foot on wood, one on water, all sun dashed
on ice. Underneath, the screaming breaks
that belt out movement shrill an unkind hymn
of praise, composed on the feminine underbelly
by those who worship by taking in their mouths
blood other than water, body other than ice.

I accidentally slit myself open with a large silver knife
and brighter flowers come tumbling out, writhing
in the first cold breaths of air and unblooming.

You said you would steal a small boat when the time comes
to leave. That way you must say goodbye only to the sea.
How is it you alone know the time? And why
would you say goodbye to the only one you want to join?

Long, blackened hands will enter
the first fold of the sea and join with others drowned
to establish a greater deformity; a female body washes
ashore. The ice clouds are brighter than the life is.

My vocal patterns fade without flowering.

The flown river woke in black
caricatures of birds hunched forgotten
on the bank where winds are harvested—
pulp of feather, the twenty thousand
born into ancestral ammonia six weeks past,
bones broken beneath the aggressors' weight:
the man who has thwarted his instincts,
who has seemed to escape because of the body
it is someone's profession to masturbate.
To perform what is necessary, he sews
skins by machine. I will be killed.

So I bleed rain, you have noticed. You move me,
your standing pain. If you go on crushing the silence,
my love becomes impotable, like answers
dust rushes on, a blue river, a stone you wear unwinding.
We know the bellies of blackbirds.

If all the times that I have waited
wanting to be alone
the birds on my shoulders bear down
the birds have been heavy
on my shoulders,

and the hills so long to look back
and my shoulders turn into strong wind,
humble branches
seem to sway above,

where my mind's eye is a nest
and the mind is an egg
warming like eggs in the sun's old light,
and there is no one—

birds sound small
• *about to crack open so a welt can emerge:*
the wound that created the world
but wind thrushes the throat;
decayed black years enter the voicebox
and detonate.

As she grew heavier—so that she could stay
on the earth and keep the soft dirt on her feet—
her dress was embroidered with stones

all the colors in grey and edged with eyeteeth
she could read and that could read the salt drops
from the minute holes in her skin sounding
against one another—and together—as they walked
the sky back down and, once affixed there, held on,
smoothing the sun, holding the heat to her fingers
so that she would always have someone to talk to.
And when they finally reached the stream,
woman and stones were lost together.

I called out to the water.
Your revolver was gleaming
beneath the first layers
of dark children.

The night-watcher's duty
was to notify the sky
of her changes in color.

You believe water is at peace
because he taught that water purifies.
But I see also that she has little rest.

A woman must suffer as she drinks
must wail as she cuts
must suffer as she prays

must scream as she gives life
must suffer if she will do
anything but live—

My father bought me this coffin,
but now I will give it to you
if you wish.

I reached in my pocket and found there
a pointer finger enfolded in an old-
fashioned handkerchief and lavender.

You shook your head as I handed you
everything inside. You spat your wisdom
teeth at me from the back of your throat.
My canines were missing.

Amazing that we cannot see ourselves as aged,
whitened, wrinkled; instead, we trace the lost
pigments back, speck by speck, from where each fell
and find ourselves at the beginning of this incarnation—
a song in a lost bird's mouth.

The cartographers lived to see
the completeness of gesture
accomplished in no one.

The commanders pitted madness
against madness, calling one logic.
Now my body's native sounds
are mispronounced into words.

Asphalt, gravel accent, slowed stones.

If I ever cause you completely
to forget what you are about—
because I am a woman and am not
allowed to be alone without sound,
the moment drawing farther from water,
the well, the chill of Lake stoned over
again—toss another stone.

Did we forget the warrior
was inscribed under the synonyms
for Go(o)d? The grindstone has gone
bronze with aggrieved touches, wronged
like water. She keeps on. Our stories rasp
so many coils and crosses. The ending
is now: the warrior drowns

in the charming pond of bright cherub
fishes, with his shirt on, his hands groping
for something he thinks he lost, he thought
ought to be his. The stories tell him it was

a woman's breast, her neck, her wrist,
moonblack, all swallowed in the great
strong stride of the gentler orange fish.

One who is truly good at thinking
is a body unfinished
feeding herself to the dream
who practices prophecy in choirs
of chains. A clanging persists:
angels who have forgotten the way
the soul speaks—body of trees
both softer and harder than stone.

You died too soon
before I could ask your blessing
of our smile dead in the wrong places,
uneven. The pain of great cities shrivels
on our watch, as the watch of two
without eyes. We appear
like brother and sister. We are light,
yellow. You are real. We appear
to apparitions as one lost in a wild place
of blue fog and ivy. Will you hold my hand
in between times when I was more perfect
and you were alive?

I think you were happy. Then I cannot recall
your laughter. Only the unmarked distance
in the eyes. Dreams of better illness, of days

behind dense hospital windows on the unit.
A walk in heaven was limited to the number
of steps permitted. As though joy can be felt
only when counted: a unit.

Do you remember now how it was to be you?
I was a living child learning fear
firsthand, and then second, body part
by part. What kind of child are you who
must forget? I remember now how I was,
who I am covered in dark fur
drinking the light; the dust rises from all
the recent books, colors subsumed and aswim;
the snow from all directions, disoriented
grey; and so on. You did not want to touch
me yourself. You did not want to touch me,
so touched everywhere I was not,
everywhere it hurt.

You would release me now if you could, return me
to the rain in which you discerned the body breathlessly
moving, all streaks of color unfinished—anything but one.

No one comes close to the scent of you,
the odor I will wear over skin like a raincoat, smothered
plastic and pungent. The insects we become
and the creature who gnawed you slowly unholy
with equal parts gravel and light—

careful. When you could not wake, you rose
to day because it also breaks.

In the potency
of the mutilated stranger
others can recall your laughter, at least
whether the sound was blue or yellow.

True, I only suspect those colors. True, I have only
myself to remind me. What began to create, out there
in the Lake amid the bodies of the dead grey gulls
and stone copses, in the secret language, the poem
amid turmoils of light tosses unfinished.

⁓

An accordion cuts, unsettling twilight;
distortion and sunrise start early. Solitude
above and below suspends dying waters.

A man's voice enters in layers. Yellow
waves of winter follow an aged book
written before arctic eyes, witness
to the loneliness of cold, pure and complete.

Forlorn forms cling to distance, trembling
after solid breaths and being. Before the frozen
Lake we want to be warm for a moment,
flickering shades too far to touch.

We are a cold fire together. Lost
in the yellow room, I am frosted breath
on verglas, indistinct: love. Nothing changes.
Postscript some hard whisper insinuates,

you cannot exist without us—and so we return
to words as to the only home we will remember:
the one that whips us, fleshless.

This is how we hurt: linearly, in steps
that cannot be solved by lines. Across the face
the brow itself no longer is crooked and wise
but straight. This is the way the world hurts,
and still we insist she wears us:
fragments of river
cut color, unbloom.

Even the prepositions should be to intend.
As I am prohibited philosophy due to
my sex, I am required to write of
rather than for.

Sex is such a funny thing. Why must you conceive
such serious poems, Lakes? As though you feel
we must first be bored and only then sense
the unwritten parts: anything more gold and beholden.

You in your sickness
inside green-gold vein,
the frame of best flesh,
and I in my affair with the floor.

Let us forget

as so many coils of hair pile upon the dead—
uncut
and still growing
from their opened heads.

It does not matter on what surface you write:
living skin or dried tree, bullets ground to ash.
You will always be a different animal the next time.
The conflict is this. I do not want to be a woman;
even worse is to be a man. I am a creature better.
But neither cat nor dog, the only two humans let
into their homes. A nameless creature moves best,
leaves no enduring shapes. I don't call any one
God. How could we really be close? And in these
moments warmed with blood one person has only
torso. One has only hands or a foot. We contort.
We start to see, on the faces of the women men find
beautiful, beards. The trick may be to inhabit the skin
we have completely, to wear it without nails, to trust.
Trust in me completely.

I have all these dark years before me
to harvest your shadow
more deliberately
and decipher what thin webs will say
above the corners,
to ask the spiders in the cave
what color their light is.
And all the time these women with visions
walk around crucified,
and the fruits of the orange tree
are sweetened by our blood.

At the redoubled crucifix
six sweet tastes dance,
three of flesh and three
of nothing. The last one
wears a skin and seeks another
who sees before as clear
as voices that come this way
down a lovely hill trembling.

Hummingbirds still fly by the beaded orange fruit in rain;
they dip down, grey, and fall up, their own green lights—
above the burial tree, thick rain so heavy on the small wings,
the eyes crushed open.

The rain-soaked pages wet my dreams,
illegible in the morning, returned
to water—the most beautiful
thing I have ever written.
A forest's long sigh.

Under the softly bleeding moon,
moisture, ecstatic in blue-green
pools, separates us from its skins of gold;
a happiness I hold exudes rote hope
and love in red and death.

You said once to me, an apparition:
grow your hair to hide behind,
a curtain. Become for the birds
a nest, closer to gold than to rust,
closer to dirt than to men.

Every day, I tear down a steel building with bare fingers
and bright blue arteries to expose the heart,
find the contours of dark—inside beautiful, endless blackbirds.

I became pregnant from the wind that is said
to drive the mountain dwellers to madness.
I come from the blue moment between skies.

The dark insects of happiness, anonymous
as they fly and fall—the dreamscapes never
permeate my blood: I grow cold and shiver
through the night. Ants meet and exchange
scents. Into the scree the ropes fly and birds fall
from black jaws. The sweet-smelling flowers
were vultures over the dying one, hovering—
A story about death is also a love story. A cloud
breaks. Is it possible? Yes, our baby is growing
on my dreams. Perilously, I make mostly
nightmares, digested long before the colors
reach my mind, empty except for the blackbirds
frozen in ice. A drop hits the floorboards
and the ants rush back in their holes to tend
the divinations, to hush the red spark. Any attempt
to understand is a translucent hand bent before
the thaw, stirring the nameless ones we have lost.

A restless creature crawls from the damp floor
with broken feet to shelter in my mouth.
She likes to feel my unformed words on her wounds
and the sting of my salt, which she licks like soft
blood. It reminds her of the Lake, safe
from the lashes beneath.

A strong love, a strong hurt.

She slips inside my stomach with a purpose
to be there when I wake and when I sleep,
without dreams. She intends me to give birth
to her soon, to send her into the world in a new way
—in reverse, into a land that does not look out
over hell but floats on dark water.

I tell her she is not even in the right place—
who gives birth from the pit of the stomach, as to a stone?
She says, *you do,* and she finds in the crashing waves
that begin too soon a beautiful blue insect.
The cockroach emerges: a perfect glimmer
in a hardened night, polished by my pain.

In this way, before she is gone
in the rush of broken tissues and strong blood,
we have created the only beauty strong enough
to survive the world.

Filled with unresolved stars
like a cloak of holes,
streaming stray light
onto the scene of a crime
long forgotten,
a birth.

Echoes off the red brick walls
radiant from sun and heat—

Children's cries smashed
on the cobblestone drive—

Old screams reverberate now
in the soft stone chambers of my mind,
with one room for each of the dead.

Sense in the straps holding me fast
to the bed, someone who loves me,
a stranger who believes my blood
should be higher, a tide on which
dreams of a dead child can float

into the mouth of God, on the same red
sound the forgotten ones wailed
when ships still lay at the bottom of the Lake,
the silt bed where we all have rested,
a skin both strong and soft that slips away
to show us the choking cold,

everything we cannot believe in the warmth:
the black beneath, the depths of the love
the living harbor for the dead,
especially those who have been us—
crying out for help—or have died in us
before they could swim.

We see them surfacing—broken, skin-
colored shells a young doctor silently
scrapes from my cervix.

Down a dim corridor dusted with mute light
through thick double panes,
like a stream passing in slow motion,
women glide one by one: ghosts
with sheets shrouding their fragile frames.
Always covered, their bodies like girls, their faces
like fruit bats, you can see each delicate bone
by the patches of sun through the films of wing
stretched tight to cover the valuable inside.
They shift before the cold metal threshold,
where a man behind a door waits to vivisect them,
desperate to hear the last words of the martyred
saints that fill their empty bellies.

This is a love poem, black water.

To defer to men and gods
with large speculums and weak minds—
the black water would never forgive us,
and we would grow sick on green winds

and scared enough to hide our dead
below ground
where no one may see their enduring
sorrow over our hasty lives
or their changing expressions
as they transform into God—
the omnipresent virus who imprinted us
with our genomes, who wrote our DNA
from special characters known to other
creatures and not to men.
All ages are steeped in strong
estrangements. Shamed ones
drown in the remorseful pools
of their own eyes.

Cannot hide in the stories you tell yourself
or the people called Carol
or in your memories, smoldering in pools
of muted light, no doorway out.

I wear my ghost feathers
from when I was a bird,
a better creature.

They nailed my mind to the cross
but left the rest of the body free—
creating this confusion.
The captive ideas haunt the dirtier corridors,

the mind and autumn lights,
the leaf left undecayed for thirty years,
the shadow intact.

The medieval facets of my mind are illuminated:
the great space between words writes sharp clouds
with sides impaled on the glimmering number.
Over the deeper blue glacier, the wise-muscled
deer of ice and unbroken space breaks the cold.
The articulated heart plunges through the darkest
word into deep gold blood, unclaimed.

The womb is ablaze with a burning crown of words.
Spider is the soul personified.

The way from elaborate suffering is not up but in.
As I force my action into words, return my words to action.

The hunger to compress matter is to petrify sunlight
into delicate yellow birds you can clutch but not eat.

The fragrant desert is a dead ocean in the key of blue.
When they give hunger to God, have humans forgotten
the way the soul speaks?

Small spider sounds, small spider lights.

Your desert is burning
while you are lying
prostrate as in prayer,
your chalice slanted
beside you, the sacred
blood spilling down
your legs. Relinquish
the tempting memories,
the pain, and your love
for your burning land,
and you may learn
to live again.

It was snow, blue and sunken, with the bearing
of powerful waters that gave me this shape—
swallowed and drowned, one chill halo encircling
the mallard neck; it returned me, mouth and iris
in blue rings, a form that held water and shifted
underweight. Underneath a shining layer of ice,
I lived, deep as darkness, my frozen roots,
my frozen teeth, and the fingertips pressed blue
to the transparent sheet. The two glass points
that gleamed from beneath were the stars of drowning:
they found heat to bury us—but alive, alive, a Lake.

Stirred by love, the frozen clouds may separate, drift,
obscure the wreckage impaled on black cliffs, but we stay,
mouth pressed to white panes. The frozen birth of my perfect
sound rushes up through ice, and the ice from our eyelids
breaks, lash by crashing lash into more perfect pains.

When I go home I get lost in a room.
This room is where I am crazy.
This room is outside time.
This room is where St. Vitus will cure me.

In the dirt you have discovered emptied eyes,
you believe, but images engraved so long ago,
like yellowed stains on the retina, still burn,
too hot to tamper with. Memories manufactured
for them will singe your fingertips in turn.

Then you can take a bone from my body,
whittle from it a city or the wings
for a broken mind—golden flicks, tissue-
thin—thick with perspiration, heavy
black heads that droop, break, and lie dying
in pools of dying light. It was a weapon
already, a whiteness, clean. A relic.

Rooms give way to dreams of rooms,
lonely nests sharpened in black winds
nurtured by ghosts who dream of graves
serious in ice.

The dirt collapses at the summit;
below us the wall of bodies speaks
through us. They tell us everything
we will forget.

Someone shackles the grey dove's
legs with the lightest silver chain;
it shines for a moment as she flies
away.

The yellow room never left me;
there never has been a question
of an open window or a way outside
my false suns' arctic halos. In my sleep
paralysis I run to you, the ghost
of me: soft child with hair illuminated
entangled in hard thoughts.

She never has left the yellow room;
she always has been drifting outside.
If we turn now, the shadow of a woman
centuries old shall press plague-black

lips to our mouth, kissing us
with the conjunction of three planets.
The bacteria inside the swells outlive us.

Silver people slip in and out, waiting to kill me.
Slim, with limbs like smooth tapeworms, they bend
and fade in the light. Nothing obstructs them.
When I find myself drowning at night, I call out
to the ice. The future depends on whether
a coyote or a small, dark bird answers me.

Our autobiography reads like this: hundreds of tiny suns,
a hummingbird creating the flower worlds, a pain perceived
from underneath. The guilt I have fermented is an antidote,
a trade I learned apprenticed to my father. From his mother
I learned to read the light bent through glass beads into colors
of suffering in the many mouths of rivers. Smoke escapes
unhindered through the birth canal; guilt-glass clouds tilt
perilously from that sky. My mother's mother taught me
to live in mud where it is clean, where our toes sink deeply,
flexing to hold us up. She knows the coyotes and hears
their runes, although the ancient silt and respect for the waves
ensure their furs pass only in the dead of night: whole worlds
and a perfect love for the cold brimming from a white horse
she carries on her back. What power and dark she anticipates.
She is there, at the edge of the lived world.

Underwater, something bright stirs. Beyond
reach, I am dizzy. A wave issues from the abdomen,
and the ice spreads. I am caught beneath the cold
without the chance to scream or blink—
a piece of tin fills slowly with loose snow.

My grandmother's coyote, a shadow, snaps up
the spilled child in his jaws, pads past my eyes
frozen open, crosses the black edge. The forest
closes. In the end, or right away, we weep
but only for the living.

The soft rain of my childhood descends
into my eyes, becoming ever longer bodies
of water I am quite sure I have never been
before. I am someone else's river
just as I have been someone else's rain.

It is quiet now in the dim yellow light
of afternoon, early or late in life.

Just as the sound of wet sky spoken
through water is silence, awash in fresh
silver, it is hard to say just the right flower.
So much blood just to make the right verb,
muddy and pure, as though sweated
from the souls of the feet

in the most amorphous moment
of the strongest movement when all parts
of grass, air, green, bird, body of water
have come apart and come apart.

When I run bare of the river bank, a dress of mud rises
and cools the thorn scratches. The throat is a rose. I am
a dying man. I do not dare to touch the river's face
with my perilous stillness.

The nightingale wakes and I am on fire, streaked silver.
The dream has given fire to empty eyes. The hair
of my grandmother has grown past my icy feet. The age
of children is at rest,

at play with woodcuts and blocks of death purposefully
dulled at the edges. The headache grows. The eyes augment
until the photographer has something worthwhile for his images.
I turn around the silver spool.

I, the spider who gave threaded birth to the silken moon,
I the boy who dies too early, I the bird who cries outside of time,
outside the glassless window pane but does not pass—
and I, the woman

in the earth who releases the river and breaks reigns:
this is my love—and the river, forbidden inside—and when
the river touches the first toe I burn to nothing and am
no more.

How long does life last, though? No
real measure makes the rain any longer,
growing the green river on the skin.
The time left, the moments you decided
with green clarity to save, you can count:
one ink flower,
one woman,
one kiss,
one gravel pit
beside a sparse highway,
one question
that always returns you.

Beside yourself with glorious, secret questions,
an emaciation of equations and bouquet
of phrases you say to yourself but attribute
to the dark, you try to choreograph

walking in a line, and it cannot work,
though the body balances better, weighted
as it is with sorrow; the line does not exist.
Like a map of your uterus, it can hold

no weight. It feels like your brother's last
skin cells permeate the cold in the walls,
disrupting the semblance of stillness
you found so disturbing. The cells

breathe through the damp to speak with you
in a different temperature and a language
you do not yet understand: yellow.
In the house of great sorrow

and stagnant pools of holy water, you shiver,
and the birdbath stands empty. Dust hovers
in a vacant corner crumbled to light;
sorrow and day draw pale smiles across

the expanses of green decay, faces gone
to seed. Birds blown to attics in flusters of oil
and paint beat their wings and cannot move.
They see new soil dry to dust, and the question

that hovered before the eyes in July seemed
to have migrated somewhere with water
but just reappears in the mirror. It was behind you
all the time, supporting your head, holding you up

or back. This is the language of peace that decomposes
us who are said to be alive, possessed by names
and numbers, until our fundamental parts begin
to pulse at last—unseen organs, cells, colors speak

the same questions that animate him, unbounded
by our limits and lines and indemnified against words,
including that catholic sign for a far-reaching land
that pious men call "the dead."

Prone to dreaming the contours of a god
he could not trace, a man was like stone
but without the thought or flowing water.
It was as though God were dead to him
and a man rose from His grave.

I would have been enclosed in a cell,
for my safety of course, from the wrath
of that god who designed a girl from cloth,
all pink and without blood. Then he calls
for a sacrifice, and as in tag or guns, I am it:

the one who attempts to touch
the skins of friends and is left to her own
vigorous movements until she comes to feel
that even her good, pulsing blood is frantic
and she has caught the dancing sickness.

But that god is perplexed.
He remembers putting nothing inside.
He is horrified that in the emptiness
he created for her, she keeps a shining
blue insect and a dancing death.

Even the bed quakes with the wrath
of men's dreams. What is the source
of my infection? Something lying inside

the color red? *What do you want to be*
when you grow up? they ask the child.

A ghost.

How frequently it is the most threadbare detail
tucked away in a corner of the mind, in a corridor
blocked by dust and sand, and embarrassment
or shame, and filled with a memory that does not age
but strikes just as strongly as the initial experience
when one accidentally steps into herself and dies.

Her edges of comprehension are too sharp
or too much thought rests bleeding in the hands.
Let the flies light up as they pass through
the severed thoughts. The cold acres of hair wave,
crisp last lettuces, last light through the threads
before the sky slides closed.

I hear underneath the ice not just the memory
given me by my ancestral dead as gifts
through waves, but with my head this time.
Between recitations, the dead still talk about
it, whispering through mouths
full of stones in my half sleep,
the days of anger swollen at the throat.

If my hands are drawn to the stones
I carry you around like my only ghost,
and everyone believes and knows
the only equals the most holy.

The way your light bites me,
the wounds your shabby halo inflicts—
September and I have lost the name
of the month in my mouth—September,

and I have lost in my mouth
the way the edge undulates,
the power of conversion
where the rocks are jagged,

the words unpalatable. The people
have lost the name for the month
and misplaced the location of memory:
the tongue that flicks the entrance

to the underground, the pathway of all
animals, the way the green no longer
resembles that green we thought
we knew. You wanted to touch,

but your fingers only passed through.

You slept with a rope
or a bible under the pillow
in self-defense

and dreamed of the stories
that would martyr you.

God's lover, I slept with
my hands beneath my pillow,

until they were cut off
at the wrists, and I left them

behind with the other stigmas
and my plague.

With handless stumps, we lift
small children, offering them
sky, but like us

they insist on going back to earth,
where the house is being built
in reverse. Soon there will be
nothing to touch.

The stones have made deep nests for themselves.
They draw comfort from the great age of earth.

The nuns dedicated to damp stone
keep vigil over the ecstasy.

And the ones who were
missing from the records
like the dignitaries of song
entered your country's chosen
autobiography—a mouth
gaping broken, opened
into the narrow street.

A hymn in a silence
free to break,
to inherit my servitude:
adore the living body
composed of cells eroding
in the direction of some lives.

What the worm carries to be devoured
is gathered around two fountains:
the orange remains of butterflies
and rusted knives plunged in water.
Be seated on words; the devoted
always wait there, hanging, ready to rise.

How many times does the name change
per breath? The dark side of the house
cannot cast shadows. Duty, separation,
and death are the same there.
But promises overshadow, circle
the wooden bowels as they necrose.

Who is afraid to enjoy such freedom—
to allow herself not to be haunted?

I believe in the nun I once was, gathering rituals
as grains gather grains of sand to themselves.
The ghosts of who I am now cry out, lament us,
drawing to the present where my silver
body milks their sadness, waves of which
crash over us unable to move our arms,
tethered as we are to surf. We are shaken.
A glass of milk left upon cold asphalt froths
and glows. Visible now are the black materials
of sleep we dream against.

I am also the old man I drowned
in search of the silver strands.
I do not want to recall bound senses
in wires, blackbirds cast in irons.
Speak words of ash and rust. I felt.

I could no longer live in this world.
Faces break around every corner;
every gravestone is a ship in stillness.
The words rise trees. Those buried
as women rise as bodies that move
without epoch.

And the angel I recall has no arms
and the yellow light is decayed lace
and the heat from the heart pillow is damp
with its stuffing carried out by the cockroaches
on their backs, a long time back,
and the shell is not armor, as the skin is not armor
but a drum that bursts when a voice thrashes out.

I am among the faceless, the ruins of their rooms
and great stone house, the dead toy horse. My head
is ghost white, and so I am allowed to stay. Inside
opens the longest fear, a corridor to a great black
soul like a beetle shining in the dirt. And in the mosaic
of cracked toys, colored tiles, arabesques shattered blue,
and sharp, strong plants some call weeds, my eyes
are two fragments of tile, two more shards refracting
the Lake glass damp with blood.

The jar of Lake-glass gleamed
when we needed it. The spiders came
and went. Cockroaches, do not worry.
I caressed you. I could have been more
careful. I grew up old. I was she
in the Lake. Then, I remember, I lived
in the house of color. People praise
the eagle, but the crow has known
fire and speech. Who has known water?
That is what I turn to. And God said,
What I borrow from you becomes more
than words; from you I take the memory
of my birth—a kind of water
in which nothing floats.

Oral tradition is fact: transmit the mountain.
Incant the beginning, legendary voice
gone to forest. Enchanted from mouth to mouth,
a rivulet suspended from lips becomes the phrase
we are made to breathe.

When we lived in the world of our forefathers
what was named Sin was a spot graven
on her brow in indelible furrows,
borrowed against the grape harvest,

changed for a woman beaten and buried
by the hillside, the amber necklace broken, friendless.

She lived but gave birth alone; when it was time,
she cut the umbilical cord with her teeth.
White sisters drifted
in a rosary, a whip.

The priest's work was to hold up the chalice.
The illuminated chapel belonged to him
without killing, or being killed.
Yet blood filled the cup.
He only had to say the words.

These are the exile songs of the home country.
To contribute to a more joyful exile—
the blood is her blood—
I wrote it all in my mouth,
where the mountain is only black
boulders and skilled teeth.

We are not alive when writing, but we are alone
just as no verb to be is. She writes down the truth
as it changes, and it is crowded in your mind,
you believe.

With these words you do animate me,
upon the shore washed in memory, cast
nets of tangled light and white motion.
In this morning we need not hurry.
You left your shadow to cover the mouth
when it speaks of love, the corridor
to the moment

in which we dissolve,
in which we are darkest,
in which we dissolve—

you who woke me from the dream
can take me back. In the black depths
of the soundlessly deformed, fish
rest and drift on contorted waves,
on mud, on finest silt. I thought
you were dead. How is it I talk
with you who have never been?

One of us is lying with words, clouds
drifting nowhere with thoughts dangling
from orifices of rain. Remember me: only
space.

Open.

You wear your words well,
I am told, like a great-grandmother
in a frame or an aged gentleman
who instructs the broad daylight
in Latin at noon precisely
to a light once scarlet no longer
glaring against but with us.

As the hours progress
so do the faces worn by the dead.

The dead near.

The hem of the undergarment catches on a gap
in wind and air where their breaths are. We drink
water from ourselves, twisted in soundless agony,
the juniper berries shriveled inside the bird
whose suspended swoop is as the day is long.

But not long enough.

I felt when a piece of the same sea washed over
me on the beach you loved me in absences. Polished
like stones, the body of days glistens. The moon
is a host on the tongue.

You decay in me.

With pink gashes, the unhealed sky repeats
the longest grey sleeps. A tree cuts slantwise
the white-stained bank, reflection throbbing
the calm surface. Above you, in me, long ago
like an unborn being. All beautiful animals

once loved the crepuscule taste on my still,
bright teeth. Alone on the bank, in the lateness,
in the surf, in the Lake in the wood, in the wake,
you decay on my tongue,

unfinished.

A brown moth came to me
alive as dust
to remind us how it is
to live for one day in the dark.
Stay on my forearm; I will
love you from the distance
of mouth to wound,
the scarred wind always
whipping the soles of our feet,
stinging and cooling our way
to perdition.

You can find the past in the river of fish,
the rattle of guts filled with teeth:
rain inside cactus. I fed them words
ripped from our mouths, the love last.
Between black word and water glides
a corridor, inside the fish, where the moths
who made flame are born brown.
You can find it in fish: past the carp's mouth
lies anything lost; past the old boat
the black erased shame lies like a haze.
Ply the river higher; carp upon carp rattle.
Inside fish, letters drop from bile-sharpened
cliffs, shattered clouds, and splintered
woods intended to drift. The first time
the jagged semi-voices touch our skin,
we itch and then burn the silences.

Who will tend the pink fire?
Uncovered memories in a basket stoke the orange sky.
Blue smoke from the burning mountain bares
grave teeth. Metal beads squeeze from human pores.
A shadow shatters silver. My armor is made of silk
spun by cockroach and spider. The creator must eat
to stay alive, even though he is older than the softest

sandshapes; water comes last and first. The same serious
ivy-shattered castle filled with human meat and musk
rises for the stars to feed on before their sacrifice.

Cormorant, bury the dead now in the mouth. Who speaks
for whom? Sand village entrance: the wind lost in the larynx
again chokes on black, star particles, starfish as light as water
and as dark. Moon cracks; the life of the sky suffers space.
Discover the pebble, the silver hair from the scalp of the new
fishes; no direction is ever lost; every direction is never wrong.
Seek in the streetlight or turn it off, turn to mix the spine.
Invite the cat to spill truths. As long as the mountain range
is spilling, leaping, I have borne myself! Newly learned
waterfalls spill scissors; leap, cutout fishes!

Until the guilty among the voices scream,
until the voices are extinguished of burning angels,
until their white stars, frigid with rain feel you in the fields,

you bend over your body fighting like fish on dirt.
Their rapid decay walks on across burning gold,
swelling like death with spotted skin.

Lovers stroll with no power, relinquishing
the right to stop, licking the lips of unexpected infants,
to suck in their voices before they take their first breaths.

They must know him first and believe he is God.
A string sharpened from a green thread glosses from a snake
hidden in distance. Long ago the garden grew over

the derelict fence without gate, opening into an opening.
This was the afterbirth of death after the fortieth death.
It condemned the voices to the cradle, the grating

from which to recognize love and begin to vine upward,
as the sheers guided us, in madness as in rain—
he has built this sanctuary for the dead around us.

In such temperatures and such trials of ice
and strength, only the dead have the chance to escape.

During his time, he used words as though firing
rapid and sporadic bullets,
making misshapen the air and ghosts around him.

He evidently never learned to speak of ice as ice does.

The cold wooden house the Lake breathes beneath
swells and exhales from the deep brown gardens
of dogs asleep, the soft-tongued love of salt
and life, and the echoed chop of knife against board.

Sacred and real, the grey priest performs
the ritual and his right: devouring the body
of Christ. Steel grey ships weaken, cross
open palms, and gulls etch signs into dark.

The beauty of sighs steams from the ancient
cup, gold reflections of the blood across knife—
sharpens the love, dulls the stars. The endless
winter preserves the memories of a life.

My grandmother calls the Lake her God.
She cares for the wind and the saints
we starved on the floor, early in paradise,
never older than Christ.

Fresh water is life.

God likes it, likes us. God loves
only God. How much are our stars
to blame for being our stars? With cold
holes for words, they turn and swerve.

There is a sacred space between
their cup and our parched lips.

God stays, a little bit drunk.

Is it possible that I have killed someone before? At night
I recall thudding the head over and over with open palms—

blood of dreams, broken knives. This hand is the culprit.
My right hand will be tried for murdering in the absence

of the left. It must be exhausting pretending one of us is not
a man, seeing sinister halations of faces imposed over mine.

Is that why you close your eyes? Remove the aspect of two
planets from your head. The trigon spans upward
and is darker than the darkness.

Today is your birthday, and you are dead.
Now the clouds overflow—rain on the little
flower, snow on the little flower. Grey touches
every surface except the still yellow petals
sheltered among the vacant fingers—yellow
in the drops of water that form and fall away—
always untouched.

I still check your notebook from time to time
expecting to see some new words written there
though you died years ago. Someone has to look
for new signs, perhaps a clue submerged in a shape,
or a note I did not recognize every other time.

I never enter sleep anymore—but find myself
in the world of the dead, wandering the streets
bright with the sunshine of a certain yellow mood
that appeared only in my childhood.

What gives it away is there are no shadows,
and the sun is so strong in yellow triangles
and overflowing streams yet cool on the white
pavement where we linger and play.

From someone behind a bright yellow funnel I accept
a gift, but the letters are illegible unless they cannot be
read by living eyes. I must keep going back to look
through the full streets where the ghosts were young
and holy and first abandoned.

The sound of snow
through the rain
magnified—silence
explodes. I love you.

I am growing birds inside me;
a flock of feathers crops up
red and glowing in my darknesses.

What the birds say slips under
roots woven in new ways, spoken
like snakes slowed across light years,
as yet unheard.

We do not receive the blackbird
we desired but are left standing
with half our blood.
The longest serpent stirs
bright stones around our legs.

The constellations on your back
speak when we need them.

A starry sky and a December day
shake us to our knees
until the bones tremble
and shine; illuminated from inside,
they reveal the relics they will become.

Grandma continues to incant
the rosary with the television voices
after my heart drops into the toilet.

God's silence?
I am sorry.

When the *products of conception* crush out,
unrecognizable except to us, great heart-sized clots
continue to pulse, organs shuddering on the sterile
floor, converting the cold to sun-cracked ice.

I cannot stop weighing the hearts in my hands:
slivered masses of meats, raw and delicate,
that slide between my fingers as they expand
and contract. I raise one to my lips.

The corpse fills my hands with bright red wounds.
Half my insides I hold like an offering; half cascade
down the legs. The gown glows red. The fingernails
drip without sense as the cuff repeats its squeeze;
lights continue to seek a pulse.

The red holes in my palms as the *residual
materials* are forced from me are too large
to be stigmata, yet I am marked from head to foot.
A woman wipes away the blood I shared, confesses
Now you are clean.

I begin to tell you the bedtime story again, and you are dead now.
I still speak as though I know some things. More words
will betray us. More accurately, we betray them in us.
And words shape the way some would like to mold our childhood
into memories, into shining shapes, to remember walking straight
and sunny paths, to encourage us. I am wary.

The time has come and come.
I no longer write the love poem.

The birds came up in order. The oldest and youngest
lifted a wing and brown shadows emerged, webbed
curves chasing air into ether, the arcs that make the world
and the shadows that bear down on our lids, sustaining
the dreams of good things—namely, that the world
is a safe place in which to wake.

I dreamed I was you
and woke up dead.

Acknowledgments

Cholla Needles: "The birds of prey have gathered together...,"
  "As it turned out, his guardian angel...," "The doors to the
  rooms hang open now..."
DeLuge Journal: "The dark insects of happiness, anonymous..."
La Piccioletta Barca: "When I was at war in a childhood...,"
  "You can find the past in the river of fish..."

About FutureCycle Press

FutureCycle Press is dedicated to publishing lasting English-language poetry in both print-on-demand and Kindle (eBook) formats. Founded in 2007 by long-time independent editor/publishers and partners Diane Kistner and Robert S. King, the press incorporated as a nonprofit in 2012. A number of our editors are distinguished poets and writers in their own right, and we have been actively involved in the small press movement going back to the early seventies.

We award the FutureCycle Poetry Book Prize and honorarium annually for the best full-length volume of poetry we published that year. Introduced in 2013, proceeds from our Good Works projects are donated to charity. Our Selected Poems series highlights contemporary poets with a substantial body of work to their credit; with this series we strive to resurrect work that has had limited distribution and is now out of print.

We are dedicated to giving all of the authors we publish the care their work deserves, offering a catalog of the most diverse and distinguished work possible, and paying forward any earnings to fund more great books. All of our books are kept "alive" and available unless and until an author requests a title be taken out of print.

We've learned a few things about independent publishing over the years. We've also evolved a unique and resilient publishing model that allows us to focus mainly on vetting and preserving for posterity poetry collections of exceptional quality without becoming overwhelmed with bookkeeping and mailing, fundraising activities, or taxing editorial and production "bubbles." To find out more about what we are doing, come see us at www.futurecycle.org.

The FutureCycle Poetry Book Prize

All full-length volumes of poetry published by FutureCycle Press in a given calendar year are considered for the annual FutureCycle Poetry Book Prize. This allows us to consider each submission on its own merits, outside of the context of a traditional contest. Too, the judges see the finished book, which will have benefitted from the beautiful book design and strong editorial gloss we are famous for.

The book ranked the best in judging is announced as the prize-winner in the subsequent year. There is no fixed monetary award; instead, the winning poet receives an honorarium of 20% of the total net royalties from all poetry books and chapbooks the press sold online in the year the winning book was published. The winner is also accorded the honor of being on the panel of judges for the next year's competition; all judges receive copies of all contending books to keep for their personal library.

www.ingramcontent.com/pod-product-compliance
Lightning Source LLC
Chambersburg PA
CBHW070011100426
42741CB00012B/3194